TRIBUTES

BLACK PEOPLE WHOSE NAMES GRACE SEATTLE SITES

TRIBUTES

Black People Whose Names Grace Seattle Sites

By Mary T. Henry

Forward by Mayor Bruce Harrell

Illustrations by Marilyn Hasson Henry

Second edition
Published by HistoryLink
Produced by HistoryLink
HistoryLink.org
206.447.8140

Author: Mary T. Henry
Illustrator: Marilyn Hasson Henry
Foreword: Mayor Bruce Harrell
Book Design: Marie McCaffrey
Editors: Nick Rousso and Tori Smith
Production Assistant: Kiku Hughes

ISBN: 978-1-933245-66-9
LCCN: 2022946860

This Book is Dedicated to My Family.

Contents

Foreword

As a young college student at the University of Washington, I was first introduced to the concept of the 'griot tradition' watching the television series *Roots*. Defined as an oral history spanning years and generations, it's how African people passed on the accounts, records, and stories of their communities, cultures, and ancestors.

In *Roots*, author Alex Haley presented a reconstruction of history using that same approach. In fact, the griot tradition has been one of history's most effective tools for ensuring culture is passed down to the next generation — even in the face of a systemic campaign to eliminate that culture and those stories, through slavery, disenfranchisement and discrimination. The griot tradition has allowed our stories to carry on, to demonstrate resilience, and to inspire the next generation of leaders, families, and communities.

It's a notion that is similarly rooted in the ways and traditions of the people who have been here and cared for this place since time immemorial. In my political work with tribal communities and Indigenous people in the Northwest, I have been told rich stories and understand that elders are held in high esteem, in part for their incredible ability to pass on traditions, culture, and customs.

This tradition has brought us family histories and family traditions, stories of loss and stories of triumph, books and movies, facts and legends, intimate understandings of people and places.

I recall hearing the stories of my own family, passed down by my grandparents and their grandparents, traced back to Louisiana and Japan. It may manifest in different forms, but we know that this same idea — this same approach to storytelling, to record-keeping, and, most important, to community building — is found today in African American communities including here in Seattle.

Today, in Seattle, the naming of our public spaces — streets and parks, buildings, and institutions — allows that same tradition to continue, and to grow. In the griot tradition, many Black Seattleites know the impact leaders like Edwin T. Pratt and Homer Harris had on our city. With wonderful parks named in honor of these leaders – Pratt Park, Homer Harris Park – we recognize that so many others who don't know these towering figures will ask questions like 'Who was Edwin T. Pratt?' 'What did Homer Harris do? 'Why did they matter?'

It's these kinds of questions that drive further learning, that drive improved historical consciousness, that drive better understanding of the diverse and longstanding communities that make this city special.

This considerate thinking and research, and these thoughtful questions about those we don't know, transcends race and ethnicity, religion, or background. It helps bring us together to understand shared history and shared experience.

While Seattle has grown over the past several decades, in wealth and in population, that same Seattle has become less Black as our community faces increasing pressures of rising costs and gentrification. It's our obligation to do our part and uplift and elevate the stories of the Black community members who helped shape Seattle. To memorialize and revere those stories and moments, so that culture isn't lost. The way our ancestors preserved stories and persevered through challenges unimaginable today.

There are many Black pioneers who haven't been recognized, who persisted and endured through systemic racism and personal trials. Stories like those of the Henry family, who refused to accept exclusivity in the form of redlining and helped change the course of Seattle's history in simple pursuit of a place to call home.

We know preserving our history goes beyond a name on a sign or a link to a webpage. It's about understanding the people and the struggles they faced, the ideals they held true, the actions they took to accomplish a better future for their neighbors and for their community, then and today.

As Seattle's second mayor with roots in the African American community, it's my honor to follow in Mayor Norm Rice's footsteps. To know our stories and to use real history and lived experiences to determine priorities. By being intentional, we can make the most of the opportunities in front of us through the policy decisions we implement and the investments we make. We can build the kind of equity and diversity we want to see in this city. To build *One Seattle*, ensuring this is a place for all communities as a welcoming city filled with opportunity.

There are future stories to tell and names to celebrate, but only if we choose to learn from the leaders of the past, to share their history and apply their lessons. That's why I'm grateful for this book, the stories it tells, and the thousands of people it will empower to share these same stories for generations to come.

Mary T. Henry's leadership, conviction, and dedication to the contents of this book about Seattle is worth high praise. I am humbled by her tenacity, and, as mayor, will always see her as one of Seattle's most treasured historians.

—Mayor Bruce Harrell

Introduction

The face of a city reflects the hopes and dreams of its people, their ideals and their heroes. Nowhere in a city is it reflected more than in the names of its landmarks. Our Seattle streets are named for early settlers and national heroes; our parks and school buildings are named for people who in some way have made a contribution to our area or to the nation. Yet, in our daily rounds of the city, we cross these streets, and pass parks and buildings bearing names that we take for granted, never knowing their significance.

In 1997, I published *Tribute: Seattle Public Places Named for Black People*, which focused on 22 people and their landmarks. This book is an enlargement and includes information on 53 individuals and the landmarks honoring them. It is intended to paint a picture of these individuals so that as you pass the landmarks, they will come to life for you.

In writing this book, I was constantly amazed at the contributions these people made to the life and culture of Seattle, the nation, and the world. Alice Ball, a native Seattleite chemist, made a major contribution to the treatment of leprosy. Denice Hunt, an architect, is responsible for the appearance of Benaroya Hall and Westlake Park. Quincy Jones and Jimi Hendrix have brought pleasure to people around the world through their music. Many others contributed to the quality of our lives through sports, literature, music, education, politics, and healthcare.

Some of the people included were friends and acquaintances of mine: Dr. Blanche Lavizzo, Jean Shy Farris, Judge Patricia Clark, and Judge Charles Stokes and his family. Edwin T. Pratt sat at my family room table with me, and Ivan King designing the Triad Plan to desegregate Seattle Public Schools. Gertrude Peoples is still a treasured friend.

Of the 53 individuals honored, 10 are Seattle natives including the Gayton Family, Alice Ball, Dr. Homer Harris, Jimi Hendrix, Peppi Braxton, Larry Gossett, and Jacqueline Lawson; three are Garfield High School alumni: Ernestine Anderson, Quincy Jones, and Hendrix; 10 are internationally or nationally known. Though some of these individuals came to Seattle from various places in the nation, their lives in Seattle made an indelible impression on the city.

Hopefully after reading this book, and when you drive down the streets of Seattle, rest in her parks, and pass her buildings, you will know why they are so named. My apologies for any sites that may have been overlooked.

—Mary T. Henry

*Number in parenthesis below biographical material indicates reference citation

Acknowledgements

I want to thank my students at the South Shore Middle School, where I was librarian during the 1970s and 1980s, for alerting me to the fact that they were unaware of the people for whom the places they visited were named. This is what inspired me to research and write *Tribute: Public Places named for Black People*.

Georgia McDade and Stephanie Johnson Toliver, President of the Black Heritage Society, were early supporters of this project and in fact were the impetus. Many others were helpful in my research. They include Juli Farris, Annette Hall, Risa Lavizzo Mourey, Stephanie Stokes Oliver, Seattle City Clerk, the Meredith Mathews family, the Al Larkins family, Seattle Department of Parks and Recreation, Seattle City Archivist, and librarians at the Seattle Central and Douglass-Truth Libraries.

I am grateful to my daughter-in-law, Marilyn Hasson Henry, a retired Epiphany School teacher, who insisted that I write the narrative for this book and that she could do the drawings; to my son Neil Henry, Dean Emeritus of the School of Journalism at UC Berkeley, who, with a critical eye edited the manuscript and was so patient and encouraging; to my son, Bob Henry, retired Lakeside School history teacher, who was my able technical support and leg man for pursuing a publisher; and to my grandson David Henry for providing input. My daughter Sharon Henry and granddaughters Risha Mary Henry and Mira Hasson Henry were standbys with loyal support. Indeed it has been a family journey.

Finally, I am grateful to HistoryLink, the online encyclopedia of Washington state history, an institution I have worked with since its founding in the late 1990s. They donated the design, editing, proofreading and publishing of this book in recognition of my contributions, and dedication to HistoryLink.

—Mary T. Henry

Clarence Acox Jr. (b. 1947) was leader of

the Garfield High School jazz band for 40 years. He was born in Louisiana and attended Southern University in Baton Rouge. After being recruited by Seattle Public Schools, he arrived in Seattle in 1971. For the first few years he directed the marching band at Garfield, and, by 1979, he had formed a jazz band program at the school.

The Garfield jazz band began traveling around the country, competing with other high school bands and winning every competition in Nevada, California, Idaho, and Washington. The Essential Ellington High School Jazz Band competition in New York is the largest competition in the country, and Garfield's Jazz Band is the only band to take first place four times.

One of the most influential music directors in the nation, Acox has received many honors. In 1991 he was named Musician of the Year by the Earshot Jazz Society of Seattle. *Downbeat* magazine named him Educator of the Year in 2001, and in 2003 he was presented the Impact Award by the National Academy of Recording Arts and Sciences. Seattle's Cornish College of the Arts awarded him a Doctorate of Fine Arts in 2016.

Acox and Michael Brockman are cofounders of the Seattle Repertory Jazz Orchestra, and as an accomplished musician, Acox has been enjoyed

ARCHITECTS
RENDERING

in Seattle's club venues. He retired from Garfield in 2019 but has been a major influence in JazzEd, a nonprofit educating young people in music.[1]

Clarence Acox Jr. Way is located in Rainier Valley on South Hill Street between 21st and 22nd Avenues South. The street honors Acox for the work he has done for the youth of the city and the work he has done with JazzEd. The Seattle City Council approved the recommendation on July 13, 2021. A multiuse building to house JazzEd will be built to welcome students in grades 4 through 12.

Ernestine Anderson (1929-2016) was a jazz and blues singer

who performed for over 60 years. Born in Houston to a music-loving family, she grew up listening to her parent's blues records and to her father, who sang bass in a gospel quartet. She entered a local talent contest when she was 12 years old. Because she tended to improvise the melodies of the songs she sang, she was described as a jazz singer.

When she was 16, her family moved to Seattle, where she enrolled at Garfield High School and graduated in 1946. In 1952 she auditioned, backed up by the Ray Charles trio, for a spot with Lionel Hampton's band. She was hired and toured for 15 months. In 1958 she performed in the first Monterey Jazz Festival and was featured on the cover of *Time* magazine.

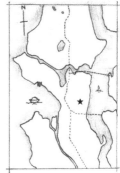

She had a bout of depression in the early 1960s, but recovered by 1976 after her conversion to Buddhism and learning the practice of chanting. A few years later she had recorded 14 albums. On Quincy Jones's label she released *Now and Then* and *Blues, News, and Love News*, both of which were nominated for Grammy awards.

Anderson performed at jazz festivals all over the world, including five times at the Monterey Festival. She also performed at Carnegie Hall and the Kennedy Center. Her singing voice was versatile, ranging from romantic to earthy. She died at the age of 87 in Shoreline, Washington.[2]

Ernestine Anderson Place is located at 2010 South Jackson in Seattle. The colorful building has 60 studio and one-bedroom units, with 30

reserved for chronically homeless seniors and 15 for the elderly with low incomes. Counselors and mental health services are on site.

Ernestine Anderson Way was approved by the Seattle City Council in a resolution on August 17, 2006. There are honorary signs on South Jackson Street between 20th Avenue South and 23rd Avenue South.

Alice Ball (1892-1916) was a pharmaceutical chemist credited with

producing the most effective treatment for leprosy into the 1940s. She grew up in Seattle, the daughter and granddaughter of Seattle's first Black professional photographers. She was exposed to the magic of chemistry while watching them develop photographs.

She attended Seattle High School, the city's first high school (located at the site of Broadway High School and Seattle Community College) and graduated in 1910, with top honors. Graduating from the University of Washington in 1914, she earned two degrees, one in pharmaceutical chemistry and one in pharmacy.

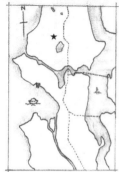

One year later Ball isolated the active ingredient in chaulmoogra oil, which provided relief to leprosy patients. After receiving a graduate scholarship from Hawaii College (later the University of Hawaii) she became the first woman and the first African American woman to receive a master's degree in chemistry from the school. She was also the first woman to teach chemistry there.

Alice Ball died at the age of 24 during World War 1. While demonstrating the use of a gas mask in Honolulu, she accidentally inhaled chlorine gas, later causing her death. In 2000, the University of Hawaii acknowledged her as one of its most distinguished graduates. [3], [4]

Alice Ball Park is located at 81st and Greenwood. It is a pleasant greenspace for children and adults. On a corner with easy access, it has a looping path, natural play elements, and a gathering plaza with comfortable seating. The park opened in June 2019.

Powell Barnett (1883-1971) was born in Brazil, Indiana, and moved to Roslyn, Washington, in 1889. His father had been among many Black miners recruited to work in the coal mines of Washington. As a teenager, Barnett also worked in the Roslyn coal mines and played in the "colored" band.

Powell Barnett came to Seattle in 1906 because he thought the city offered greater opportunities. He began working for Barary Asphalt Paving Company as sub-foreman putting in new streetcar lines. Later, he worked for the General Engineering Construction Company, which built the Waldorf Hotel at 7th and Pike and the Perry Hotel at 9th and Madison. He served as a clerk for State Senator Frank Connor and retired at 71 as a maintenance man at the King County Courthouse.

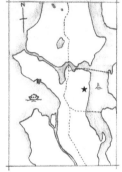

A man of many interests and great energy, much directed toward improving race relations and civic unity, Barnett became a leader in the community. He organized the Leschi Improvement Council and became its first president in 1967. He led in organizing the East Madison YMCA and served as chairman of the board. Barnett chaired the reorganization of the Seattle Urban League, thus preserving its membership in the Seattle Community Chest.

A sousaphone player and a firm believer in racial integration, he was instrumental in uniting Blacks and whites in the YMCA, the USO, and the local musicians' unions. He was the first Black person to become a member of the once all-white Musicians Union, Local 76. A star baseball player, he organized a semi-pro baseball Umpires Association in Seattle, served as its executive secretary from 1944 until 1961, and secured affiliation with the National Association of Umpires.

Barnett received numerous awards for outstanding civic contributions from many associations in the city, including the King County Council on Aging, the Jackson Street Community Council, the Seattle Urban League, as well as from the mayor and city council. [16]

Powell Barnett Park is located on Dr. Martin Luther King Jr. Way between East Jefferson and East Alder in the Leschi Community. This large, well-used park has something for kids of all ages.

Roberta Byrd Barr (1919-1993) was a

woman of multifaceted talent – civil rights leader, librarian, TV personality, actor, journalist, and the first woman in the history of Seattle Public Schools to head a high school when she was appointed principal of Lincoln High School in 1973.

She was born in Tacoma and attended Tacoma's Lincoln High School. At the University of Washington, she earned a B.A. in Sociology and Elementary Education as well as an M.A. in Librarianship. She taught in Seattle Public Schools at Jefferson and John Muir as a librarian.

Her acting and TV career began in the early 1960s when she starred in *Raisin in the Sun* with Greg Morris at the Cirque Theatre in Seattle. She told stories to children in a show on KCTS/9 called *Let's Imagine*. Later she moderated the program *Face to Face* on KING TV from 1965-1970, and from 1971-1972 on KCTS/9. The program aired before a live audiences and featured guest speakers discussing controversial topics such as desegregation and welfare. She awakened the community to civil rights issues and other important topics overlooked in the media and acted as a bridge between the Black and white communities.

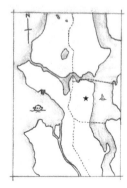

In 1966 she was appointed to the State Board Against Discrimination, and in 1968 she was appointed vice-principal at Franklin High School, after 150 students held a sit-in to protest the expulsion of Black female students wearing their hair natural. In 1973 she was appointed principal of Lincoln High School. She was an active participant in the Urban League, the NAACP (National Association for the Advancement of Colored People), and her sorority Alpha Kappa Gamma. [5]

Byrd Barr Place at 722 18th Avenue was once known as CAMP (Central Area Motion Project) and Cornerstone. It was renamed in 2018 and dedicated to carrying on the legacy of this amazing woman. It continues to extend help in housing, food, and other services to those below the poverty line and from various social, cultural, and ethnic backgrounds.

Peppi Braxton (1963-1971) was a first grader
who was killed on his bicycle after he sped down a
driveway into the path of an automobile on Yakima
Place South.

Although Peppi lived in the Colman Elementary
School area, he attended kindergarten and first grade at
Leschi Elementary School at the request of his parents.

He was an attentive, alert
student, admired by his teachers, and a favorite of
the other students. A teacher called one day to tell
his mother, "The children look to Peppi to lead them
and to take care of them." The students at Leschi
voted to have their playground named for him. (16)

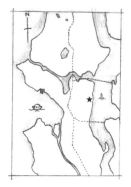

Peppi's Playground is a delightful patch of green,
east of Leschi Elementary School between East
Spruce Street and Lake Dell.

Odessa M. Brown (1920-1969) was a

community organizer for the Central Area Motivation Program (CAMP) during the 1960s. She was a staunch supporter of a healthcare facility for children in the Central Area.

She worked in the neighborhoods to make residents aware of the needs of the area and to express these needs to the planners of Model Cities. Brown was a quiet, private woman, but when she spoke, people listened. It was always about healthcare for children. So it was that when the Model Cities presented its health plan, it was for a children's clinic.

Born April 30, 1920, in Des Arc, Arkansas, she came to Seattle in 1963 as a licensed beautician, having trained in the Madam C. J. Walker Beauty school in Chicago. As a mother of four, she worked hard to support her family through work in the Central Area Motivation Program and as a beautician at Les Coffie's DeCharlene Fashion Beauty Salon at 2105 East Union.

Friends and associates were unaware she suffered from a debilitating illness. When she missed a meeting or did not report to work on rare occasions, no one assumed anything more than a minor problem. It came as a surprise to all who knew Odessa Brown that had suffered from Leukemia for much of the time she had been associated with CAMP.

Odessa Brown died on October 15, 1969. When the time came to name the children's clinic when it opened its doors in 1970, there was never a question from the organizers but that it be the Odessa Brown Children's Clinic. [16]

Odessa Brown Children's Clinic is a satellite of Children's Orthopedic Hospital offering medical, dental, and other support services for all families regardless of their ability to pay. It has two locations, one at 2101 East Yesler Way, the other at the corner of South Othello and Martin Luther King Way South.

John Cannon

(1914-2014) was the first director of Odessa Brown Children's Clinic in Seattle's Central Area. He had a distinguished U.S. Army career, first serving in the all-Black 555th Parachute Infantry Battalion, also known as the "Triple Nickels." After 24 years of service, including his time in the Korean War, Cannon retired as a lieutenant colonel.

Returning to Seattle from Korea, Cannon became a founding member of Seattle CORE (Congress of Racial Equality), serving on its Emergency Committee. He also worked in the City's Division of Urban Renewal for two years before assuming directorship of Odessa Brown Children's Clinic. He worked closely with Dr. Blanche Lavizzo to provide quality care with dignity to the patients.

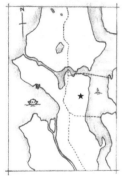

Cannon later became Executive Director of the Ecumenical Metropolitan Ministry, and served from 1980 until 1988 as Executive Director of the Central Area Senior Center. He served on many boards including that of the Seattle Public Library. During SPL's campaign Libraries for All, Cannon was featured in a film at the Douglass Truth Branch Library depicting how central libraries are to communities, and encouraging financial support. [29]

Cannon House Assisted Living is located at 113 23rd Avenue South. It has been in operation since 2009 providing care for retirees, seniors, and others in need of residential care who want to live as independently as possible.

Randolph Warren Carter (1913-1970) was a

Seattle social worker who developed a sheltered workshop center for developmentally disabled individuals. His sheltered workshop project started out in an old warehouse building on South Jackson Street. There, with the use of simple machinery, an enrollment of 10 to 15 trainees was maintained. Some of the trainees were referred from Pacific Prevocational School, a Seattle Public School program. Gradually it expanded to provide on-the-job training for mentally, emotionally, or physically disabled people as well as job placement and vocational training.

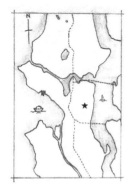

From this simple beginning, the workshop known as the Central Area Industrial Workshop was started. It was licensed under the State of Washington and received grants from the federal government. In 1976, the property at the corner of 23rd Avenue South and East Yesler Way was purchased through the City of Seattle, and a new home for the facility was constructed using grants from the federal government and individual contributions. After Carter's death in 1970, the facility was named Randolph Carter Industrial Workshop.

Carter came to Seattle after receiving his master's degree in Social Work from the University of Southern California in 1952, and launched a successful career. He served as Community Relations Secretary at the Seattle Urban League for three years, then moved on to become Juvenile Probation Officer for the King County Juvenile Court from 1956 to 1959. In 1965, he was appointed Executive Secretary of the Washington State Board Against Discrimination. [16]

Randolph Carter Center opened in 1988 as the Catholic Community Services at the Randolph Carter Center after the industrial workshop was forced to close in 1986 due to diminished federal and state financial support. A portrait of Randolph Carter and a plaque about his life hang in the lobby of the building.

Horace Cayton Sr. (1859-1940), a former slave,
came to Seattle from Mississippi in the late 1880s and began publishing *The Seattle Republican*. It was directed at both Black and white readers and at one point had the second-largest circulation in the city. He was married to Susie Revels, the daughter of Hiram Revels, the first and only Black person elected to the U.S. Senate from the state of Mississippi.

After emancipation, Cayton enrolled in Alcorn College and graduated in the early 1880s. Realizing his education and will to succeed could reach their real potential if he left the South, he headed West. He ended up in Seattle and worked as a political reporter for the *Seattle Post-Intelligencer* and later for a Black newspaper, *The Seattle Standard*.

Seeking to publish a paper that appealed to both Black and white readers, he published his first edition of *The Seattle Republican* on May 19, 1891. According to Cayton the paper stood for right, championed the cause of the oppressed, and advanced the success of the Republican Party. He was active in the party and obtained important positions.

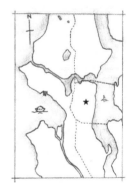

However as the Black population increased so did prejudice. He lost his influence in the Republican Party and important party positions as time went on. In 1917, Cayton published an article about a Southern lynching. As a consequence, subscriptions to the publication were cancelled and advertisements dropped. He lost his beautiful home at 518 14th Avenue North (now East) on Capitol Hill, where he had entertained celebrities including Booker T. Washington. He continued to pursue a career in publishing and issued *Cayton's Weekly* from 1916 until 1921, but was unable to make it an economic success. [6]

Cayton Corner Park is located at 18th Street and East Madison. It is a small plot of land with a concrete wall once emblazoned with newspaper replicas. It is a work in progress.

Patricia Clark (1945-2015) was appointed

King County Superior Court Judge in 1998 by Governor Gary Locke. She was a strong advocate for alternatives to incarceration of youth and the disproportionality of sentencing youth of color. She supported Drug Court and Family Court as the way to help young people in trouble.

She obtained her Master's in Public Administration and a law degree from the University of Washington. She was in private practice before joining the King County Prosecutor's Office as deputy prosecutor in the Criminal Division. She developed expertise in the Struck Jury Selection Method and taught it to attorneys across the state.

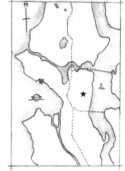

After leaving the Prosecutor's Office, she accepted a teaching position at Seattle University Law Clinic. She remained there for two years. In February 1996 she was appointed to the King County Superior Court bench as a Constitutional Commissioner. Her primary focus was on cases involving at-risk youth and children in need of services.

Judge Clark sat on the statewide Gender and Justice and the Minority and Justice Commissions. She was a member of the Superior Court Judges Association and served on its Education Committee and the Family and Juvenile Law Committee. She was involved in developing the Master Plan for Juvenile Courts in the twenty-first century.

She was on the Girl Scout Totem Council and the Municipal Golf of Seattle Board. She was the coordinator of the Youth and Law Forum. [7]

Judge Patricia H. Clark Children and Family Justice Center, dedicated in 2019, is located at 12th Avenue South and Alder Street. The new building replaces the old Juvenile Center with a more progressive program emphasizing therapeutic services.

Thelma Dewitty (1912-1977) was the first Black
teacher to be hired by Seattle Public Schools in 1947. Her
hiring came after intervention on her behalf by the Seattle
Urban League, the NAACP, Civic Unity Committee, and the
Christian Friends for Racial Equality. Her first assignment was
at Cooper Elementary School in West Seattle.

Born in Beaumont, Texas, she graduated from Wiley
College in Marshall, Texas. Though she had taught in Texas for 14 years,
segregation policies there prevented her from continuing her studies.

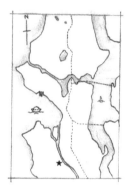
Because of this, the state of Texas paid her tuition to the
University of Washington, and she decided to stay in
Seattle.

During her first year at Cooper Elementary School,
white teachers were told that a Black teacher would join
them and anyone feeling uncomfortable about that could
transfer, but no one objected. One parent asked that her
child be removed from her class, but the principal refused
her request. Dewitty also taught at Laurelhurst, John Hay,
and Sand Point elementary schools, and finally at Meany
Middle School.

Her affiliation with Cooper School was one of the main
reasons the school was granted landmark status by the Seattle Landmarks
Preservation Board. The site is on the National Register of Historic Places
partly due to her.

Besides teaching and working with the NAACP as president of the
Seattle Chapter, she also served on the Board of Theater Supervisors and
the Washington State Board Against Discrimination. [8]

Thelma Dewitty Theater is located at 4408 Delridge Way Southwest
on the Youngstown Cultural Center, formerly Cooper Elementary School.
The theater has 150 seats and hosts theater productions, film screenings,
and community meetings.

Dewitty Room is
located on the mezzanine
floor of the Graduate
Hotel at 4507 Brooklyn
Avenue Northeast in the
University District. It
is primarily a room for
meetings.

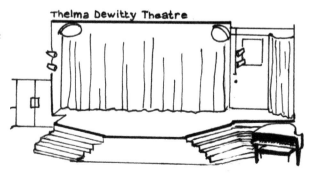
Thelma Dewitty Theatre

Frederick Douglass (1817-1895) was born

a slave in Tuckahoe Creek, Talbot County, Maryland. In slavery he led a very hard life, sleeping on the floor, wearing few clothes in winter, and fighting over food with the dog. The daughter of the plantation owner found him appealing and arranged for him to be the companion of her nephew in Baltimore. There he learned how to read and write and led a pleasant life. But his benefactor died when Douglass was 16 and he was ordered back to the plantation.

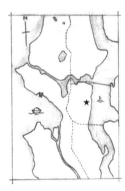

After a few aborted attempts, he escaped in 1838. In New Bedford, Massachusetts, he changed his name to Douglass for fear of being discovered by slave hunters. He met the noted abolitionist William Lloyd Garrison and began speaking to audiences about his experiences as a slave. He spoke so eloquently that some people doubted his slavery past. This prompted him to write and publish *Narrative of the Life of Frederick Douglass, An American Slave* in 1845.

Douglass traveled to England where friends there bought his freedom, and he returned to the United States in 1847, settling in Rochester, New York. There he founded *The North Star*, an anti-slavery newspaper. His home became a station in the underground railroad system.

Douglass continued his eloquent oratory and writing, concerning himself with the abolition of slavery, equal rights for women and Native Americans, and the ending of the death penalty. During the Civil War, he pressed President Lincoln to emancipate the enslaved in the South and championed the recruitment of Black men for the Union Army. From 1881 to 1886 he served as a recorder of deeds in the District of Columbia and served as United States Minister to Haiti from 1889 to 1891.

Frederick Douglass's home in Anacostia, Maryland is preserved as site of the National Park System. [16]

Douglass-Truth Library is located at 23rd Avenue and East Yesler Way. It is the repository of the African American Collection of History and Culture. [16]

Carolyn Downs (1953-1978) was born in Marshall, Texas,

and came to Seattle with her family in 1964. She attended Washington Junior High School and graduated in the class of 1971 from Garfield

High School. She was a serious student and performed well academically. In 1972, she became passionately involved with the Black Panther Party because of her fierce interest in helping Black people in the Central Area.

A lively volunteer, Downs collected donations and cooked for the Black Panther Party Free Breakfast Program, serving community dinners, worked with the clothing bank, assisted in the Black Panther Party pest-control program, and drove the Black Panther Party van to prisons for family visitations.

Downs had a warm and pleasing personality that made her popular in the organization and in the community she served. She had exceptional organizational skills and was always successful in securing volunteer cooks for the many community picnics and dinners she arranged.

She was also active in the organization of the Sidney Miller Free Medical Clinic, the forerunner of the Carolyn Downs Medical Center, and served as assistant to Elmer Dixon, Black Panther Party founder and the Director of the clinic. In addition to these activities, Downs found time to attend Seattle Central Community College. Carolyn Downs became ill in 1978 and in a few short weeks succumbed to cancer. Downs is buried in Mount Pleasant Cemetery. [16]

Carolyn Downs Family Medical Center is located at 2101 East Yesler Way in the Central Area Health Center, which also includes the Odessa Brown Children's Clinic.

Medgar Wiley Evers (1925-1963) was the

field secretary for the NAACP in Mississippi and fiercely determined to let the nation know about the atrocities committed against Black people in the South. In 1943, after serving in the United States Army, he enrolled at Alcorn A&M College in Alcorn, Mississippi, convinced that a college education was essential to his growing commitment to change social conditions for Mississippi Blacks.

While working in Mound Bayou, Mississippi, he began economic boycotts against gas station owners who refused to let Black people use their restrooms, revitalized NAACP chapters around the state, and encouraged voter registration.

In 1954, after the University of Mississippi refused his admission to law school, he became the first paid field secretary in Mississippi for the NAACP. He and his wife, Myrlie, operated the office in Jackson, Mississippi. The specters of fear and violence were their constant companions because the white community felt a real threat to its status quo. Evers determined to expose the racial oppression and frequent violence of whites against Blacks in Mississippi. To that end he investigated every crime and reported them to the NAACP national office. His investigation of the Emmet Till murder piqued the interest of northern newspapers and suddenly a national effort was under way to fight the injustices against Black people in Mississippi.

Evers was a nonviolent person who believed two wrongs do not make a right. He was on the cutting edge of change, and it cost him his life. In the early morning hours of a cloudless summer night, he drove home after a late-night mass meeting and was killed in his driveway by a single gunshot. Anger and shame spread throughout the country and turmoil erupted in the state as aroused Black people demonstrated. On order of President John F. Kennedy, Evers's interment took place in The Arlington National Cemetery. [16]

Medgar Evers Swimming Pool is located north of Garfield High School on 23rd Avenue between East Jefferson and East Cherry Streets. It was the first of seven Forward Thrust pools to be built in the city.

Jean Shy Farris (1929-1992) was a librarian and a lover of the arts. She was the mother of two daughters and the wife of Federal Judge Jerome Farris. She attended Spellman College in Atlanta and received her Master's in Library Science from the University of Washington. She had a beautiful home in the Mount Baker neighborhood and graciously hosted many influential guests as a consequence of her husband's roles as a Regent of the University of Washington and a United States Circuit Judge 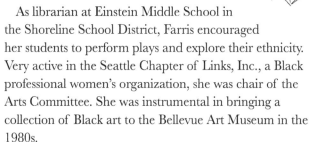 of the United States Court of Appeals for the Ninth Circuit.

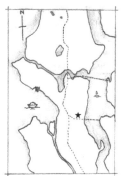 As librarian at Einstein Middle School in the Shoreline School District, Farris encouraged her students to perform plays and explore their ethnicity. Very active in the Seattle Chapter of Links, Inc., a Black professional women's organization, she was chair of the Arts Committee. She was instrumental in bringing a collection of Black art to the Bellevue Art Museum in the 1980s.

Farris was an avid bridge player and a member of the American Bridge Association and the American Contract Bridge League. She played regularly at the Central Area Senior Center and went to many bridge tournaments, bringing home several trophies. [9]

Jean Shy Farris Reading Room is located in the Northwest African American Museum at 2300 South Massachusetts.

Jean Shy Farris Reading Room

Prentis I. Frazier (1880-1959) came to Seattle in

1916 with little formal education but with an innate business sense and a desire to promote financial prosperity for the small Black community he found here, and for himself and his family.

He was born in the community of Magnolia Springs, Jasper County, Texas and at an early age he left his farm home to seek his fortune, first in Beaumont and later in Dallas. After his business ventures in banking and operating a boarding house failed, Frazier and his wife, Clara, headed north, eventually settling in Seattle, where he achieved financial success.

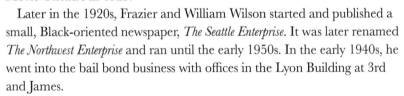

For almost 40 years, Frazier operated real estate, insurance, bail bond, and investment businesses. His first office was in the Pacific Building at 2nd Avenue and Yesler Way. Always alert to opportunities to promote other business in the small Black community, he helped organize Blackwell and Johnson Undertakers on East Marion between 12th and 13th Avenues in 1920. At 21st Avenue and East Madison, he and attorney Clarence Anderson opened the Anzier Movie Theatre in 1925.

Later in the 1920s, Frazier and William Wilson started and published a small, Black-oriented newspaper, *The Seattle Enterprise*. It was later renamed *The Northwest Enterprise* and ran until the early 1950s. In the early 1940s, he went into the bail bond business with offices in the Lyon Building at 3rd and James.

Prentis I. Frazier was an active member of the Republican Party and was a member and generous contributor to the First African Methodist Episcopal Church. He always lived in the Central Area, residing the last 10 years of his life at 410 23rd Avenue East. When the gully behind his home was designated a mini-park, relatives and neighbors recommended

it be named for him because of his contribution to the community as a philanthropist and business entrepreneur. (16)

Prentis Frazier Park is a small area filled with children's play equipment and is located at the bottom of the hill at East Harrison and 24th Avenue East.

The Gayton Family members are
descendants of John T. Gayton (1866-1954)
and Magnolia Gayton (1880-1954), who were
among the earliest Black residents of Seattle,
with John arriving in 1889.

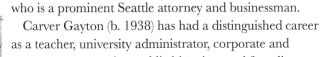

The Gaytons are among the most
outstanding Black families in the city. Notable
members of the family include Willetta Gayton
(1909-1991), who was the first Black librarian in
Washington; Guela Gayton Johnson (1927-1918),
who was the first Black librarian to head a departmental
library at the University of Washington; and Gary D. Gayton (b. 1933),
who is a prominent Seattle attorney and businessman.

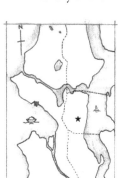

Carver Gayton (b. 1938) has had a distinguished career
as a teacher, university administrator, corporate and
government executive, public historian, and founding
Board Chair of the Northwest African American
Museum. Carver is the author of two books about his
great-grandfather: *When Owning a Schilling Costs a Dollar:
The Saga of Lewis G. Clarke, Born a White Slave* and *The
Narrative of Lewis Clarke*. They describe in detail the
hardships Clarke endured as a slave, how he was a model
for one of Harriet Beecher Stowe's characters in *Uncle
Tom's Cabin*, and of his association with leaders of the
abolition movement. [10, 11, 12, 13]

**The Gayton Family
Room** is located in the
Douglass-Truth Branch
Library at 23rd Avenue
and Yesler Way.

Russell Gideon (1904-1985) was a community

leader and a man of great energy and charm. He used these personal attributes to advantage in pursuing his many humanitarian and business interests. Born in Liverpool, Nova Scotia, Canada, he came to the United States in 1932.

When Massachusetts pharmacy schools finally admitted Blacks, he entered and graduated from Western Massachusetts School of Pharmacy in 1941. He and his wife, Lillian, moved to Seattle in 1946. He bought a drug store at 22nd Avenue and East Madison Street and operated it until 1963.

A pioneer in senior housing, Gideon built the Elizabeth James House, named for his mother, at 23rd Avenue East and East Madison Street. He was past president of the East Madison-East Union Commercial Club and the originator of the Central Area's Seafair Mardi Gras festivities. He served on numerous boards, among them Florence Crittenton Home, Seattle Urban League, Foundation for International Understanding through Students at the University of Washington, and the East Madison YMCA, where he directed fundraising for the swimming expansion. In 1963, Governor Albert Rosellini appointed him to the Washington State Board of Prison Terms and Paroles. He was charter member of the Central Area Kiwanis Club and a trustee at Mt. Zion Baptist Church.

National honor came to him as Sovereign Grand Commander of the United Supreme Council Ancient and Accepted Scottish Rite of Freemasonry, Prince Hall Affiliation, Northern Jurisdiction. In that post, he headed the 22,000 33rd-degree Prince Hall Masons north of the Mason-Dixon Line. In 1977, and until his death, he was recognized yearly by Ebony magazine as one of the nation's 100 most influential Black citizens. [16]

Gideon-Mathews Gardens is a housing facility for low-income seniors and disabled residents located at 24th Avenue South and South Jackson Street. The 45-unit building has 41 one-bedroom units and four two-bedroom units with attractive seating on each floor.

Larry Gossett (b. 1945) has been a dedicated public servant

for more than 40 years. He was born in Seattle and graduated from Franklin High School in 1963. During the following two years he moved to New York City, where he volunteered for the Volunteers in Service to America (VISTA) program in Harlem. Returning to Seattle, he enrolled at the University of

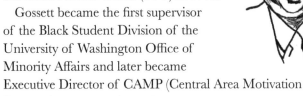

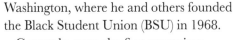

Washington, where he and others founded the Black Student Union (BSU) in 1968.

Gossett became the first supervisor of the Black Student Division of the University of Washington Office of Minority Affairs and later became Executive Director of CAMP (Central Area Motivation Program), a community action agency.

In 1993 Gossett was elected to the King County Council representing most of the inner-city neighborhoods in Seattle, and served until 2020. He was the second Black person to chair the Council, the first being Ron Sims.

Gossett fought for programs that helped inner-city youth and reduce race and class disparities in the criminal justice system. After the change of the county name in honor of Dr. Martin Luther King Jr., he spearheaded the campaign to change the county logo from a crown to an image of Dr. King.

After he departed the Council, Gossett received considerable community tribute from his constituents. He continues working in community organizing and being a force for justice. [14]

Gossett Place
is located in the University District at 4719 12th Avenue Northeast and offers over 60 units for homeless young adults and veterans.

William Grose (1835-1898) arrived in Seattle shortly after the

first settlers and became a successful entrepreneur and one of the
city's largest landowners. He opened Our House, a hotel and
restaurant on Yesler Way, which became a popular stop for
Seattle's mostly white populace. He also became a good friend
of the city's prominent pioneer families.

Grose left his home in Washington, D.C., when he was 15
and joined the United States Navy. When he left his adventures
at sea, he ventured to the gold mines in California, helped form
an underground railroad to rescue enslaved individuals, and assisted in
making arrangements for the settlement of Black people in Victoria, B.C.,
and on the Fraser River.

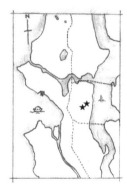

Later when he served on a seagoing vessel, the
Constitution, which carried mail between Victoria and
Olympia, he had a fortuitous meeting with Governor
Isaac Stevens. Grose found and kept safe a watch
belonging to the governor, who was so impressed with the
man he urged him to move to Washington Territory.

William Grose was the first Black person to buy
property in the East Madison area of Seattle. He
purchased a 12-acre tract from Henry Yesler for $1,000 in
gold in 1882. His home, with slight alterations, still stands
at 1733 24th Avenue.

Stories abound about his generosity, integrity, and
honesty. One story told by Attorney J. E. Hawkins recounts how Grose
sold his hotel for $5,000. It later burned in the 1889 fire. He found the new
owner and returned the $5,000. [16]

William Grose Park is a small, secluded space located
between 30th Avenue East and 31st Avenues
East and between East Howell Street and East
Denny Way. A bronze
identification plaque
with his image was
placed there by the
Black Heritage Society
of Washington State.

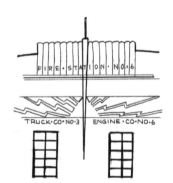

**William Grose Center for
African American Innovation** is located in
the retired fire station at 23rd Avenue South and
East Yesler Way.

Dr. Homer Harris (1916-2007) was the first

Black dermatologist in Washington and was a second-generation native of Seattle. He grew up near the University of Washington Arboretum, where he played football with friends and neighbors. Harris attended Garfield High School and became the first Black captain of the football team in 1933. Bypassing the University of Washington because of racist attitudes toward Black athletes, he attended the University of Iowa on a sports scholarship. In 1937 he became the first Black player to captain a Big Ten football team and was voted Most Valuable Player that same year.

Harris received his medical degree from Meharry Medical College in Nashville, Tennessee, and interned in Kansas City, Missouri. He chose to pursue a dermatology practice to avoid reliance on hospitals or physician referrals. He believed such a course would give him a sense of independence. After completing his training, Dr. Harris returned home to Seattle to begin his practice.

Having been refused office space in the Medical Dental Building in downtown Seattle due to the color of his skin, Harris called his friend and prominent Seattleite Stimson Bullitt about the matter. Very shortly thereafter the building manager offered him space. He became the first Black physician with office space in the Medical Dental Building.

Dr. Harris was a well-respected dermatologist with a highly regarded practice. He was honored by the Black Heritage Society of Washington State as a Black pioneer in dermatology. In August 2002, he was inducted into the University of Iowa Hall of Fame during halftime of the season opener. He attended this event in Iowa City with his grandson, his first visit to the university since he graduated. [15]

Homer Harris Park was made possible through the gift of $1.3 million to the Seattle Parks Department by an anonymous donor to purchase land

for a park in his honor. The park is located on the southeast corner of 24th Avenue and East Howell Street. Placed along a wall is an artful timeline of Seattle's Black history.

Jimi Hendrix (1942-1970) was an internationally acclaimed
guitarist and rock star who was born in Seattle and grew up in the
Central Area. He was influenced as a child by his father's extensive record
collection of rhythm and blues, by his mother's piano playing, and by
music at the Goodwill Baptist Church. As a youngster, Hendrix went to

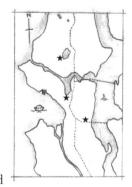

Sick's Stadium one August afternoon in 1957 to hear Elvis
Presley and watch his moves. He practiced these moves
using a broom for a guitar. When Jimi was 12, his father
traded in his own saxophone for an
electric guitar that he gave to his son
to replace the broom.

Jimi Hendrix never learned to read
music, but somehow trained himself. He
attended Garfield High School and played
in rock groups around the city. He was a member of the
Rocking Kings, which played for dances in places like
Birdland, a club on East Madison Street. Leaving school
at 17, he joined the Army where he learned to jump out
of airplanes with the 101st Airborne Division. He received
an early discharge after injuring his back in parachuting.

After his military discharge in 1963, Hendrix toured the South joining
a wide variety of acts. By 1964 he was in New York working with Ike and
Tina Turner, B. B. King,

James Brown, and Little Richard. In 1965 he formed his own group and was lured to London where he became an immediate sensation there and in Europe. His recordings of "Hey Joe" and "Purple Haze" became instant hits. By 1968 he was playing to standing-room crowds in the United States. He last played in Seattle on July 26, 1970, at Sick's Stadium.

Hendrix got his star on the Hollywood Walk of Fame in 1991 and the following year was inducted into the Rock and Roll Hall of Fame. A bust of Jimi Hendrix by sculptor Jeff Day was placed in the Garfield High School Library in 1982. [16]

Jimi Hendrix Park is located at 24th Avenue South and South Massachusetts adjacent to the Northwest African American Museum. This 2.3-acre park has an entrance with his signature sprawled in purple ink on a concrete wall.

Jimi Hendrix Viewpoint is a series of rocks at the African Savannah in the Woodland Park Zoo, located at 5500 Phinney Avenue. On one of the prominent viewpoints is a bronze plaque honoring the legendary artist and his music.

Jimi Hendrix Music Experience is located in the Museum of Pop Culture at 325 5th Avenue North.

Jimi Hendrix Statue by artist Daryl Smith is a bronze likeness of Hendrix located at the corner of Broadway and Pine Streets.

Langston Hughes (1901-1967) was an

internationally acclaimed poet who wove the rhythms of the blues, jazz, and bebop into his poetry about the life of Black people and he did it with love, humor, and optimism. He was the author of two biographies and several novels.

Hughes was born in Joplin, Missouri, and raised by his grandmother in Lawrence, Kansas, due to the separation of his parents. A lonely child living with an elderly woman in an all-white neighborhood, Hughes felt an isolation which remained with him for years and led him to express his feelings through poetry.

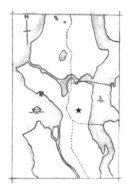

Prior to his graduation from Lincoln University, Pennsylvania, Hughes managed to publish many of his poems in magazines and two books in print, *The Weary Blues* and *Fine Clothes of the Jew*. He was one of the major writers of the Harlem Renaissance. His friends and associates included writers Countee Cullen, Zora Neal Hurston, Jesse Faucet, and Arna Bontemps.

Hughes traveled the South reading his poetry during the 1930s. His aims were to create an interest in racial expression through books and to encourage young Black literary talent. In the last 10 years of his life, he devoted much of his energy to reviewing the writing of young Black writers including the novelist James Baldwin and the poet Gwendolyn Brooks. The author John Killens gave much credit to Hughes for the "gracious encouragement" to his writing.

Hughes died in Harlem at 66 years of age. His funeral was held there and according to his instructions, a jazz band was hired to celebrate his memory. [16]

Langston Hughes Cultural Arts Center is located at 104 17th Avenue South and is a designated a Seattle Landmark because of the unique architecture of the building. It was built for Congregation Bikur Cholim when the neighborhood was the center of the Jewish community. In 1971, the building, under the auspices of the Seattle Park Department, became a center for theatrical, visual, and literary arts.

Walter Hundley (1929-2002) was a minister, sociologist, civil rights worker, and administrator of important offices in Seattle city government. He came to Seattle in 1954 as minister of the Church of the People, a liberal, non-denominational church involved in many community activities. The church folded in 1956 and social work became his focus.

Hundley received a Bachelor of Social Work from the University of British Columbia in 1960. Three years later he had earned a Master of Social Work from the University of Washington and began work at the Atlantic Street Center.

In the 1960s Hundley became a highly visible figure in Seattle's civil rights movement. As chair of the Congress for Racial Equality (CORE) and member of the Central Area Civil Rights Committee, he was a leader in organizing the boycott against Seattle Public Schools for its discriminatory practices and promoting picketing and marches through downtown for equal employment and housing opportunities.

In 1966 Hundley was asked to direct the Central Area Motivation Project, the largest community action program in King County. In 1968 he became director of the Model City Program which, under his leadership, served as a model for the rest of the country.

From 1974 until 1977, Hundley served as Director of Management and Budget for the city, and in 1977 he was appointed Superintendent of the Department of Parks and Recreation. He is responsible for the many flowers seen in a number of Seattle parks. After he retired in 1988, he worked briefly as director of the Central Area Senior Center. [16, 29]

Walter Hundley Playfield is in West Seattle at 6920 34th Southwest. The one-acre site was developed in the High Point neighborhood in 1980 and boasts two baseball fields, a lighted soccer field, a large, well-equipped children's play area, and a community center.

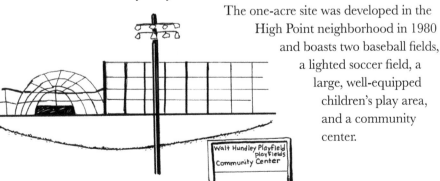

Denise Johnson Hunt (1948-1997) was

an architect for the City of Seattle. She was born in Kingston, Jamaica, and completed her education in architecture at Tufts and MIT in 1976. She and her husband, John Hunt, also an architect, came to Seattle in 1978 and settled in a home on Queen Anne. After working in local architectural firms, she began to focus on urban design and local projects as an employee of the City of Seattle.

Ms. Hunt had a major influence on the policies that shaped the waterfront, Benaroya Hall, and Westlake Park. Her efforts in bringing together resources led to the opening of the Northwest African American Museum. She was the Deputy Chief of Staff for Mayor Norm Rice. Her commitment to the community is also reflected in her service to the King County Landmarks Commission.

Denise Hunt was a member of the American Institute of Architects (AIA) and was the first Black woman in the United States to serve as president of a local chapter. As a founding member of the AIA Seattle Diversity Roundtable, she helped establish diversity programs in practice and education. AIA Seattle established the Denice Johnson Hunt K-12 Internship at the University of Washington College of Architecture and Urban Planning to support design and planning in K-12 teaching and learning programs. [17]

Denice Hunt Townhomes are located in the Greenwood neighborhood at 620 North 85th Street, close to many shops and restaurants. They were built to accommodate 10 low-income families by the Low-Income Housing Institute. There are 30 units for families with children. Families must have at least one child under 18.

Quincy Jones (b. 1933) is a Garfield High School graduate known around the world for his 70-year career in the entertainment industry as a record producer, musician, songwriter, composer, arranger, and film and TV producer.

Born in Chicago, Jones and his family moved to Bremerton in 1943 where his father had a job at the Puget Sound Naval Shipyard. After World War II, he crossed the Sound to Seattle. He attended Garfield High School, where he developed his skills as a trumpeter and arranger. Jones met Ray Charles, who was playing at the Elks Club when they were both teenagers. Quincy Jones came to credit Charles with being his inspiration.

In 1951, Jones received a scholarship to Seattle University and played in the college band. He transferred to the Berklee College of Music in Boston on another scholarship after one semester. When he received an offer to

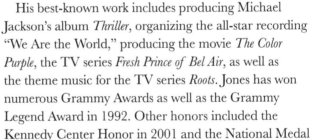

tour as a trumpeter, pianist, and arranger for the Lionel Hampton band, he joined them and left his studies. Thus began an extraordinary music career.

His best-known work includes producing Michael Jackson's album *Thriller*, organizing the all-star recording "We Are the World," producing the movie *The Color Purple*, the TV series *Fresh Prince of Bel Air*, as well as the theme music for the TV series *Roots*. Jones has won numerous Grammy Awards as well as the Grammy Legend Award in 1992. Other honors included the Kennedy Center Honor in 2001 and the National Medal of Arts in 2010. He was inducted into the Rock and Roll Hall of Fame in 2013. Honorary degrees have been bestowed upon Quincy Jones by many universities including Seattle University, the University of Washington, and Princeton University. [18]

Quincy Jones Performing Arts Center at Garfield High School was dedicated in 2006 as a state-of-the-art, 1,800-seat auditorium which boasts a green room, dressing rooms, and a place for the storing of scenery. It features outstanding acoustics.

Samuel Eugene Kelly  (1926-2009) was the
first Vice President for Minority Affairs at the University of
Washington. Prior to his call from UW President Charles
Odegaard in 1970, he had served as the first African American
President hired in the Washington State Community College
system.

Dr. Kelly had a distinguished military career from 1943 until
1966. Serving as a Second Lieutenant in World War II, he became part
of occupying forces in Japan. In 1951 he was the first African American
officer in command of an integrated combat unit in Korea. While posted
at Fort Lewis, Washington, he retired with the rank of Lt. Colonel. During
his years in the military, he earned a B.A. in history from West Virginia
State and an M.A. in history from Marshall University in
Huntington, West Virginia.

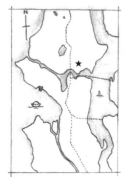

Kelly's career in education began in 1966 at Everett
Junior College. One year later he was teaching history
at Shoreline Junior College, where he developed one of
the first Black Studies programs in the United States.
As Vice President for Minority Affairs at the University
of Washington, Dr. Kelly fashioned policies to bring
thousands of students of color and economically
disadvantaged white students to the university. He also
helped the institution establish a commitment to diversify
student, faculty, and staff populations on campus. Another
of Dr. Kelly's accomplishments was securing funding to house both the
University of Washington Ethnic Cultural Center and Instructional
Center. By 1971 he had earned a Ph.D. from the university and was
appointed to the faculty of the
College of Education. [19]

**Samuel E. Kelly Ethnic Cultural
Center** is located at 3931 Brooklyn
Avenue Northeast and is part of
the Office of Minority Affairs
and Diversity at the University of
Washington. It has a wealth of
resources and opportunities available
to all students. It provides programs
and services that enhance the
communication and exchange of
multicultural perspectives and values.

Dr. Martin Luther King Jr. (1929-1968) was a Baptist

minister who shook the conscience of this nation and prompted its leaders to make sweeping changes in civil rights laws. He spoke out eloquently about the plight of Black people in the South and was inspired by Mohandas Gandhi to engage in nonviolent means for change.

In 1955, King led a bus boycott in Montgomery, Alabama, to call attention to racial segregation in public transportation. Through sit-ins, boycotts, marches, and imprisonment, he educated the nation and the world on the immorality of racial discrimination and stimulated all Black Americans to seek their rightful place in this country.

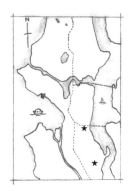

Dr. King graduated from Morehouse College in Atlanta in 1948. He received a B.A. degree in Divinity from Crozier Seminary in 1951 and a Doctorate in Systematic Theology from Boston University in 1954. He married Coretta Scott in 1954 and took over the pastorate of the Dexter Street Baptist Church in Montgomery, Alabama, in 1954.

King was one of the founders of the Southern Christian Leadership Conference and its first president. He led the March on Washington in 1963 and the Selma to Montgomery March in 1965. The coveted Nobel Prize was presented to him in 1964.

In 1968 Dr. King was assassinated in Memphis, Tennessee, by James Earl Ray as he stood on the balcony of the Lorraine Motel. Ironically, King was shot as he was reminding a musician to play "Precious Lord, Take My Hand" at the rally planned for garbage strikers that evening.

Among the Seattleites who knew Dr. King were Dr. Blanche Lavizzo, an elementary schoolmate in Atlanta, and Dr. Samuel McKinney and Judge Jerome Farris, college classmates at Morehouse College. [16]

Martin Luther King Jr. County is the most populous county in the state of Washington and is home of the state's largest city, Seattle.

The Martin Luther King Jr. Civil Rights Memorial Park is a four-and-a-half-acre City of Seattle park on the east side of Martin Luther King Jr. Way, between South Walker and South Bayview streets. The park is designed around a Black granite 'mountain,' a dramatic, 30-foot sculpture inspired by the civil rights leader's "I've Been to the Mountaintop" speech, made the day before he was assassinated in 1968.

The Martin Luther King Jr. Elementary School is in Seattle's south end between Holly and Willow streets and 45th and 46th avenues. The school serves students in kindergarten through the fifth grade.

Martin Luther King Jr. Way. In 1982, after a long struggle by Seattle businessman and activist Eddie Rye, Empire Way was named Martin Luther King Jr. Way.

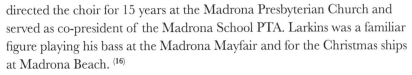

Alvin Larkins (1924-1977), though small in stature, had an enormous capacity for friendship, which he expressed through his music and in his teaching. He possessed an open, caring manner that attracted all kinds of people, old and young, white and Black. These qualities made him an effective and trusted teacher.

Born in Baltimore, Larkins did not arrive in Seattle until 1943 when, as a Naval enlistee, he was stationed at Sand Point Naval Base. He was part of the Jive Bombers, a group of professional jazz musicians there.

In 1952, he enrolled at the University of Washington in pursuit of a degree in education. His career as a teacher began in the Seattle Public Schools. For the last nine years of his life he taught social studies at Franklin High School, working closely with the Black Student Union. From 1966 to 1968. he worked with the University of Washington Upward Bound Program.

A brilliant bass fiddler and tuba player, Larkins was a longtime member of Seattle's Rainy City Jazz Band and an original performer in the Seattle World's Fair Marching Band. He was well known for playing bass fiddle at theaters and concerts throughout the area. He directed the choir for 15 years at the Madrona Presbyterian Church and served as co-president of the Madrona School PTA. Larkins was a familiar figure playing his bass at the Madrona Mayfair and for the Christmas ships at Madrona Beach. [16]

Alvin Larkins Park is located at 34th and East Pike. It is graced with a concrete path that winds through the contoured grounds lush with pine, fir, cedar, and maple trees. A bronze identification plaque with a portrait of Mr. Larkins was donated by the Black Heritage Society and placed in the park on October 14, 1989, by the Madrona Community Council.

Dr. Blanche Sellers Lavizzo (1925-1984) was

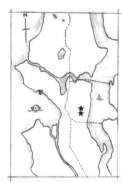

the first Black woman pediatrician in Washington and the first medical director of the Odessa Brown Children's Clinic. She was a wife, mother of four, and practicing pediatrician when she arrived in Seattle in July 1956. Dr. Lavizzo and her surgeon husband, Dr. Philip Lavizzo, left medical practices in New Orleans to pursue careers in the Northwest. Dr. Lavizzo began her private practice caring for children in her office and making house calls at night. Her presence was always a source of comfort to concerned parents.

In 1970 Dr. Lavizzo was appointed the first medical director of the Odessa Brown Children's Clinic, which provides medical, dental, and other support services to children throughout Seattle and King County. It was she who gave the clinic its motto, "Quality care with dignity." Lavizzo left her mark on the operation of the clinic, from the way the staff answered the phone to seeing that the chairs in the waiting room were comfortable.

Born in Atlanta, Lavizzo graduated in 1946 from Spellman College in that city. In 1950 she graduated from Meharry Medical College in Nashville, Tennessee. Blanche Lavizzo was a friend and classmate of Dr. Martin Luther King Jr., who visited her home during his one visit to Seattle in 1961.

An active force in the Black community, she served on the board of the Girls Club of Puget Sound and as president of the Seattle Chapter of Links, Inc., a Black professional women's organization. She was also an avid bridge player and lover of opera, a regular season ticket holder. [16]

Dr. Blanche Lavizzo Park forms a pathway between South Jackson Street and East Yesler Way. When entering from 22nd Avenue South visitors encounter an amphitheater and a large grassy area.

Dr. Blanche Lavizzo Water Play Area is located in the Edwin T. Pratt Park at 20th Avenue South and South Washington Street.

Jacob Lawrence (1917-2000) was a Harlem Renaissance

painter known for his portrayal of African American life. He was born in Atlantic City, New Jersey, and died in Seattle. His first exhibition was in 1938 at the Harlem YMCA when he was only 23. Lawrence was one of the first nationally recognized Black artists. He grew up in a Black community, was taught primarily by Black artists, and was influenced by Black people.

During his teenage years he took classes at the Harlem Art Workshop under the mentorship of Charles Alston and frequently visited the Metropolitan Museum of Art. He won a scholarship to American Artists School in New York in 1937. When he graduated, he received funding from the Works Progress Administration Federal Art Project.

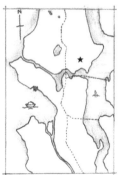

Lawrence then began creating narrative series, painting 30 or more paintings on a given subject. He completed his best-known series, *Migration of the Negro* or simply *The Migration Series*, in 1941. His other series include *The Life of Toussant L'Ouverture*, *The Life of Frederick Douglass*, and *The Life of Harriet Tubman*. Lawrence's series depicting the story of George Washington Bush, one of the earliest permanent settlers of the Puget Sound region, hangs in the Washington State Historical Museum.

He came to Seattle in 1970 with his wife Gwendolyn Knight, also a renowned artist, to teach at the University of Washington. He retired in 1983, and the couple maintained an independent unit as well as a studio unit for their continued works of art in the retirement community at Horizon House. Some of his art is displayed there. [20]

Jacob Lawrence Gallery is located in Room 132 of the Art Department on the University of Washington campus and is a living legacy of the artist's life. It features exhibits of student artwork, lectures, performances, and discussions.

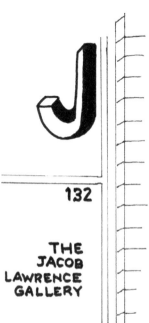

132

THE
JACOB
LAWRENCE
GALLERY

Jacqueline E. A. Lawson (1928-2021) was

born and raised in Seattle. Her grandparents, Charles and Eva Harvey, were early residents of Seattle, having arrived in 1888. She was the widow of Walter Lawson, the first Black captain in the Seattle Police Department.

Her interests in history led her to serve as an aide at the Pacific Alaska Region National Archives on Sand Point Way.

She was a founder of the Black Heritage Society of Washington State in 1977 and held many positions of the Society. She interviewed many Black residents for their oral histories and also produced exhibits for public review.

Lawson was an author who wrote, among her other works, a history of her family and a history of the Black Heritage Society. Before her death she was in the process of writing a history of the Mardi Gras Parade, a once annual event in the Central Area of Seattle.

She was the first certified Black genealogist in the Pacific Northwest and a trained oral interviewer and transcriber specializing in genealogy research. This training and experience led to six books, many articles and a curriculum entitled "Genealogy 101." She was also the co-founder of the Seattle Black Genealogy Research Group.

Lawson was a member of the Collections Committee of the Black Heritage Society and was chair for over 30 years. Her stamina, guidance, and passion inspired the volunteers who collected and archived items related to Black history and culture in Washington. [21]

The Jacqueline E. A. Lawson Resource Room is located at 5933 6th Avenue South in a building housing the Black Heritage Society Collections along with those of the Museum of History and Industry and the Puget Sound Maritime Historical Society.

John Lewis (1940-2020) was a civil rights

activist and a United States Representative from the
state of Georgia. He was elected in 1986 and served
17 terms. From 1963 to 1966, he was chairman of
the Student Nonviolent Coordinating Committee
and organized sit-ins that led to the desegregation
of lunch counters throughout the South. He also
organized bus boycotts and other nonviolent protests for
voting rights and racial equality.

Lewis was a stalwart participant in the Selma to Montgomery marches
and in the voting rights campaign. It was he who led the march across
the Pettus Bridge in Selma on what became known as Bloody Sunday. He

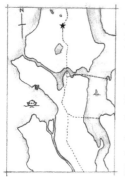

suffered a critical head injury that day when struck by a
police baton. Lewis was influential in the planning of the
March on Washington and was one of the main speakers.

In 1977 Lewis was unsuccessful in his first venture
into electoral politics. He subsequently took a position
in the Jimmy Carter administration as associate
director of the ACTION project. He was elected to the
Atlanta City Council in 1981 and to the U. S. House
of Representatives in 1988. For 15 years he repeatedly
introduced a bill to create an African American Museum,
which eventually passed in 2003.

For six decades Lewis fought relentlessly to expand and protect the rights
of Black voters and other voters of color. The passing of the 1965 Voting
Rights Act was Lewis's crowning achievement. However, because of recent
restrictions in several states, the John Lewis Voting Rights Advancement
Act aims to make discriminatory voting policies and practices illegal
throughout the United States. [22]

John Lewis Memorial Bridge opened in 2021 and crosses over the I-5
Freeway at Northgate.

Abbey Lincoln (1930-2010) was a jazz singer, songwriter,

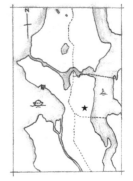

actress, and civil rights activist. She is known for her mature and heartfelt interpretations of standard songs as well as those she wrote for herself. She was born in Chicago, adopted the name Aminata Moseka in the 1970s after a trip to Africa, and died in New York City at the age of 80.

Lincoln's first album was *Abbey Lincoln's Affair – A Story of a Girl in Love*. In 1960 she sang on a civil rights recording "We Insist." Her song "For All We Know" was featured in the 1989 film *Drug Store Cowboy*, set in Portland, Oregon. For 10 years in her later life, Lincoln fulfilled a 10-album contract with Verve Records. Many of the songs she wrote reflected the ideals of the civil rights movement to inspire passion in her listeners for the movement.

Lincoln was also an actress. She appeared in the movie *The Girl Can't Help It* starring Jayne Mansfield and Little Richard, Fats Domino, and Lincoln as themselves. In that movie Lincoln wore a dress that had been worn by Marilyn Monroe in *Gentlemen Prefer Blondes*. Her appearances in other movies include *Nothing But a Man* and *For the Love of Ivy* with Sidney Poitier. In 1969 Lincoln received a Golden Globe Nomination for her appearance in the latter film.

Lincoln's television appearances include *The Name of the Game; Mission Impossible; Marcus Welby, MD; and All in the Family.* [23]

Abbey Lincoln Court is located at 2020 South Jackson and opened in 2016. It is a six-story building with 60 units. Developed by the Low-

Income Housing Institute, it serves those making up to 60 percent of the area median income for a family of four. It will help to retain racial and income diversity in the Central Area. Studios, apartments up to three bedrooms, and townhouses are available for residents. There is a common courtyard with the adjacent Ernestine Anderson Place.

ABBEY LINCOLN COURT

Alvirita Little  (1913-2006) was born on a farm in

Spring, Texas, the eighth of nine children. She walked miles to school as a farm girl. After she completed high school, she married Arthur Booker and had five children. Her second marriage was to Frank Little, a career U.S. Army soldier who retired in 1964 after 30 years of service. While stationed in Japan, Mrs. Little received her B.A. at St. Frances Catholic School in Tokyo. The family moved to Seattle in 1951 and she promptly took part in community activities.

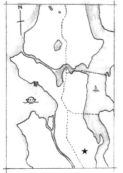

Little maintained a continuing interest in the Foundation for International Understanding Through Students, hosting 217 young people from 46 foreign countries. She also contributed her time and energy to the Seattle Urban League, United Way, Atlantic Street Center, and the United Methodist Church. But it was her association with the Church Council of Greater Seattle that sparked a dynamic and lasting legacy.

In 1969 a Black mother approached the Council with the plea from her daughter that for girls, unlike for boys, there was nothing to do, and there were no places to go. This prompted Little to organize activities, beginning with a picnic at Saltwater State Park, for seven girls. Eventually 35 girls, volunteer drivers, and community churches were involved in cooking, sewing, and swimming classes on Saturdays. Two years later the group had an organized board, served 85 girls, and became affiliated with the Girls Clubs of America. Mrs. Little served as the first executive director of the Girls Club of Puget Sound and, through her efforts, its present home on Martin Luther King, Jr. Way was purchased. It was named in her honor in 1991. [16]

The Alvirita Little Center is located at 708 Martin Luther King Jr. Way and serves girls ranging in age from 6 to 18 in before- and after-school activities throughout the year.

John C. Little Sr. (1930-1999) was a member of

the Board of Park Commissioners. His motto was "to improve the life of all people, you must improve the life of young people." Coming to Seattle from East St. Louis, Illinois, with a wife and children, he developed programs and services for the community, especially for disadvantaged youth and low-income families.

Little believed in sports competition, which offered opportunities for youth development. In the 1960s he worked with others to create the Central Area Youth Association, which expanded its services from sports to

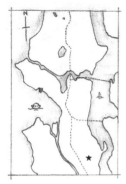

tutoring and job training. In the 1970s he helped devise a youth conservation corps for inner-city youth to train and work in Olympic National Park. Because of the success of this program, he constantly looked for ways to expose young people to wilderness challenges.

With a wife and seven children to support, Little bravely went to the University of Washington to earn a master's degree from the School of Social Work. He became director of the Mount Baker Service Bureau, which trained inner-city youth for jobs.

Little's next effort was in exposing young people to farming. He became head of the Seattle 4-H program under Washington State University and the King County Extension Program. He created 4-H programs to serve urban youth who came from families of limited income. It operated in "P patches," backyards, schools, churches, kitchens, and community centers, and became one of the most successful urban 4-H programs in the nation. [24]

John C. Little Sr. Park is located in Southeast Seattle adjacent to the New Holly Community Church at 6971 37th Avenue South. The park features a play area for children, a picnic shelter, spraypark, and a community garden.

Thurgood Marshall (1908-1993) was appointed to the

United States Supreme Court in 1967, and became the first Black person to serve on the highest court in the land. He served until 1991 when he resigned because of ill health.

Marshall was born in Baltimore and attended segregated schools. He graduated from Lincoln University in Pennsylvania in 1930. After being denied entrance to the all-white University of Maryland Law School, enrolled in Howard University Law School in Washington, D.C., and graduated in 1933, ranking first in his class.

In 1936, Marshall began a long career with the National Association for the Advancement of Colored People (NAACP), becoming its chief legal counsel in 1940. Of the 32 cases he argued in the U. S. Supreme Court

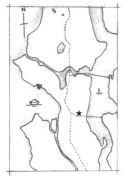

as the association's legal counsel, he won 29. Among them were cases the court declared unconstitutional: a Southern state's exclusion of Black voters from primary elections (1944); racially restrictive covenants in housing (1948); and separate but equal facilities for Black professional and graduate students in state universities (1950). In 1954, he argued and won Brown v. Board of Education of Topeka, Kansas, which declared segregated education unconstitutional.

Thurgood Marshall was a champion of civil rights and will long be remembered for his attacks on discrimination. When he died, his body lay in state in the Great Hall of the Supreme Court where over 20,000 mourners came to pay their respects. [16]

Thurgood Marshall Elementary School is located at 2401 South Irving Street and was built in 1991, as the new Colman Elementary School. In 1996, Ed Jefferson, principal of the new school, submitted a proposal to the Seattle School Board to change the name to Thurgood Marshall Elementary School. After community input the Board voted unanimously for the change.

Henrietta Mathews (1915-1983) arrived in Seattle in 1957

with her husband Meredith and two young sons. With a career in social work and a passion for fair treatment for the young and the elderly, she made a distinct contribution to the betterment of life in Seattle.

Born in Columbus, Ohio, Mrs. Mathews received her B.A. degree in Business Administration at Ohio State University, a Master's in Social Work from the University of Oklahoma, and a Master's in Education from San Jose State.

She began her distinguished career in Seattle in 1958 with the King County Juvenile Court as Probation Officer. From 1959 to 1965 she served as case worker with the Lutheran Family and Children Service and was interim supervisor of Adoptions and Field Work Instructor for students from the University of Washington School of Social Work. For the next three years she was branch executive of the East Side YWCA. Here she inaugurated a successful program that provided education for unwed mothers. This program was adopted by the Seattle Public Schools as its first continuing education program for unwed mothers. In 1968, she joined the Seattle Public Schools as coordinator of school district programs and activities related to minority racial groups. During her eight-year tenure she supervised the tutoring of low-achieving students, and coordinated the voluntary racial transfer program and the District's Human Relations Training Unit.

After her retirement she worked incessantly as a volunteer to the aged, serving on the local and national Older Women's League and the Seattle King County Advisory Council on Aging. Governor John Spellman recognized her dedication and service by appointing her to the Washington State Advisory Council on Aging. [16]

Gideon-Mathews Gardens is a housing facility for low-income seniors and disabled residents located at 24th Avenue South and South Jackson Street. The 45-unit building has 41 one-bedroom units and four two-bedroom units with attractive seating on each floor.

Meredith Mathews (1919-1992) was a friend to

youth and his name was synonymous with the YMCA. A man of pleasant demeanor and personality, he began an association with the organization in 1937 at the Spring Street YMCA in Columbus, Ohio, and continued his professional career with the organization in Oklahoma City and McAlester, Oklahoma.

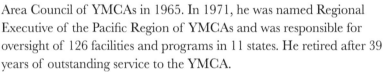

Mr. Mathews came to Seattle in October 1957, as executive director of the East Madison YMCA. The fundraising and business management skills he had developed in Oklahoma were used to expand services, memberships, and programs at the Seattle branch. A new facility was built in 1965 after a successful capital funds campaign under his leadership and with outstanding support from the community.

In recognition of his contributions to the organization and his loyalty to the YMCA family, Mathews was appointed associate executive of the Pacific Northwest Area Council of YMCAs in 1965. In 1971, he was named Regional Executive of the Pacific Region of YMCAs and was responsible for oversight of 126 facilities and programs in 11 states. He retired after 39 years of outstanding service to the YMCA.

Born in Thomaston, Georgia, Mathews received his high school education in Columbus, Ohio. He received his B.S. degree from Wilberforce University in Ohio and pursued graduate studies at Ohio University.

Mathews was uncommonly loyal, not only to family, but to friends and to just causes. He was a personal friend of Edwin T. Pratt and Randolph Carter and served on the boards of the Seattle Urban League and the Randolph Carter Family and Learning Center. In 1995, his name was placed in the YMCA Hall of Fame in Springfield, Massachusetts.

Meredith Mathews died on March 10, 1992, the result of injuries sustained during a robbery and assault in Seattle in June 1991. [16]

Meredith Mathews East Madison YMCA
is located at 23rd Avenue and East Olive Steet. A modern structure was built in 1965 and remodeled in 1991 and again in 2016. It houses a childcare center, gymnasium, full aerobic workout center, and a swimming pool.

Louise Jones McKinney  (1930-2012) was a

philanthropist, patron of the arts, educator, and principal of
several Seattle Public Schools. She was born in Cleveland,
Ohio, and graduated from Case Western Reserve University.
She married Reverend Samuel B. McKinney and moved to
Seattle in 1958.

During the height of the civil rights movement, she began making lasting
improvements in the education of Black and disadvantaged students. She
joined the Seattle Public Schools teaching corps and advanced to principal,

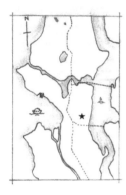

all the while emphasizing attention to the achievement of
these students. She encouraged and pressured institutions
to ensure that those capable children got an equal chance
at educational opportunities.

She was founder of the Mount Zion Baptist Church
Scholarship Ministry and co-chair of the Mount Zion
Scholarship Fund, which gave thousands of dollars to
worthy students. She was also actively involved in the
church's preschool and kindergarten, and later the Ethnic
School that became known as the Louise Jones McKinney
Learning Center.

McKinney served on the boards of a number of
nonprofits in the area of education, child development, and healthcare,
including Town Hall and Bailey-Boushay House. She was also active as
a board member of ACT Theatre where she encouraged diversity in its
offerings and was involved in the creation of a playwright program for
junior high and high school students.

She was a partner with a group of minority women who operated several
businesses in the Seattle Tacoma International Airport. In 1994, she retired
from Seattle Public Schools as Director of Academic Achievement. [25]

**Louise Jones McKinney
Reading Room** is located
on the ground floor of the
Douglass-Truth Branch Library
at 23rd and Yesler Way.

LOUISE JONES M^cKINNE
READING AREA

**Louise Jones McKinney
Learning Center** is located in
Mount Zion Baptist Church at
19th and East Madison.

Rev. Dr. Samuel Berry McKinney (1926-2018)

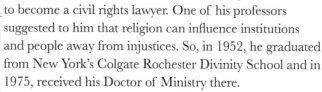

was the pastor at Mount Zion Baptist Church for 40 years, a civil rights pioneer and community leader. He played a major role in the Central Area Civil Rights Committee. He was a founding member of Seattle's Human Rights Commission and was responsible for bringing his classmate, Dr. Martin Luther King Jr. to Seattle in 1961.

Rev. McKinney was born in Flint, Michigan, and graduated in 1949 from Morehouse College in Atlanta, where he had planned to become a civil rights lawyer. One of his professors suggested to him that religion can influence institutions and people away from injustices. So, in 1952, he graduated from New York's Colgate Rochester Divinity School and in 1975, received his Doctor of Ministry there.

In 1958, he and his wife, Louise Jones McKinney, moved to Seattle after a brief period in Rhode Island. His leadership at Mount Zion led to the congregation's tripling its membership to 2,500. In addition to his ministerial role, he was a powerful force in the community.

Rev. McKinney marched in the streets of Seattle along with leaders of CORE, NAACP, and the Urban League, pushing for equal job, housing, and educational opportunities. With other Black church leaders, he was arrested when protesting apartheid in front of the South African consul's home. He marched with Dr. King in Washington, D.C., in 1963, and in Selma and Montgomery in 1965.

McKinney co-founded the Seattle Opportunity Industrialization Center (SOIC), a vocational training center, and was a founder of Liberty Bank, the first Black-owned bank in Seattle. He was the first Black president of the Church Council of Greater Seattle and served on the boards of the Meredith Mathews East Madison YMCA, the Fred Hutchinson Cancer Research Center, and Washington Mutual Bank. [26]

Samuel B. McKinney Manor, located at 1916 East Madison, is a 55-plus senior housing facility built in 1998. It is a five-story building with 64 units.

Dr. Samuel McKinney Avenue was named in 2013 for the blocks running on 19th Avenue from East Union to East Madison.

McKinney Center for Community and Economic Development is located at 2120 South Jackson. It offers pre-apprentice training programs, employment training in technology, a contract/business support center, and other relevant programs.

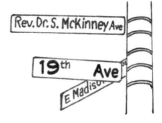

Gertrude Johnson Peoples (b. 1932) is the

founder of the country's first academic support office for college student athletes. For over 40 years she was mother figure, friend, and academic adviser to athletes at the University of Washington, where she held the position of Director of Student-Athlete Academic Services. In 1971, she hired two assistants to a staff that grew in later years to 14 members and 85 tutors.

There was much racial unrest on campus in the 1970s and she was

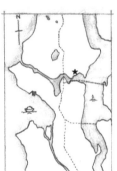

recruited by the Office of Minority Affairs to counsel Black students to prevent them from dropping out. She led the effort to see that they were more comfortable on campus by acquainting herself with the faculty, making friends, and becoming knowledgeable about every department. This led to her interest in increasing academic help to all athletes in all sports.

It was in 1973 that she joined the football coaching staff on their recruitment trips and became the first woman athletic recruiter at a major university. Her success in recruitment resulted in the NCCA allowing others beside coaches to recruit.

Two athletic awards have been named in her honor: The Gertrude Peoples Scholarship Award to a student athlete pursuing a graduate degree, and The Gertrude Peoples Award, which is given to a UW coach who has assisted student athletes in achieving academic success. In 2011 she was the first woman and first non-athlete to be honored as a "Husky Legend" at the UW-University of Hawaii football game. [27]

The Gertrude Peoples
Student-Athlete
Academic Service Area

is located in the Ackerley Academic Center inside the Conibear Shellhouse on the lakefront of the University of the Washington campus. It houses a computer lab, study rooms, tutoring rooms, and printing services.

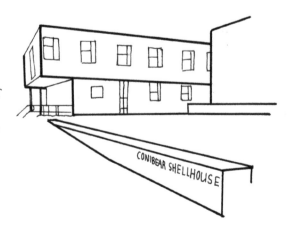

CONIBEAR SHELLHOUSE

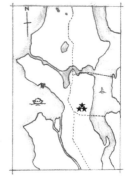

Edwin T. Pratt (1930-1969)

Seattle was blanketed in snow on the January night in 1969 when Edwin T. Pratt was shot and killed in the doorway of his home by an unknown assailant. The city was shocked by the murder of this man whose voice was one of calm during the racial turmoil of the 1960s. Funeral services were held at St. Mark's Cathedral and his body was interred there.

Mr. Pratt was executive director of the Seattle Urban League. He lived in Seattle a little over 12 years, yet his leadership in human and civil rights have left an imprint on the fabric of life in the city. A committed integrationist, he believed that the problems of race could only be solved through integrated efforts.

Housing discrimination and de facto segregated schools were in place when Pratt arrived in Seattle in 1956. Through his leadership the League grew from a staff of five to 25, and changes began to take place.

To ease segregation in schools, Pratt supported the Triad Plan, a proposal for reorganizing Seattle's elementary schools developed by an Urban League committee. The Triad Plan became a turning point and hallmark in the continuing struggle against de facto segregation and for quality multi-racial education. He also conducted quiet negotiations with the University of Washington, urging the school to improve minority opportunity.

In housing, Pratt consistently pushed for integrated neighborhoods and promoted Operation Equality, the League's fair-housing listing service, and sponsored a federal program encouraging home ownership by low-income families.

A catalyst and a negotiator, Edwin T. Pratt led Seattle on a higher road in race relations. As a local cleric commented, "His example should not be lost upon future generations who should recall his effort and glory that he once lived among us." [16]

Edwin T. Pratt Park, with its barbecue stoves and picnic tables, is bounded by 20th Avenue South, East Yesler Way, South Washington Street, and 18th Avenue South.

The Pratt Fine Arts Center is located at 1902 South Main and serves over 3,000 students and 500 working artists.

Pratt Park Apartments, located at 1800 South Jackson, is a four-story building offering many amenities, including a roof-top terrace, a 24-hour fitness center, and a theatre.

Tyree Scott (1940-2003) was a civil rights and labor leader who

opened doors for women and minorities in the construction industry. He was the leader of a group of Black contractors known as the Central

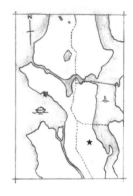

Contractors Association (CCA) who sought equal compliance in Federal building projects.

Scott was born in Hearn, Texas, and grew up there except for a brief time in Seattle where he attended Madrona Elementary School. He served in the U. S. Marine Corps during the Vietnam War. In 1966, he moved to Seattle, where his father, Seth Scott, sought to establish his electrician business in the Central Area. Trade unions were off limits to Black people, and this limited his ability to compete for large contracts.

During the months of August and September 1969, Scott led the CCA in shutting down major federal construction sites throughout Seattle to protest the impossible position of minority workers. Their demonstrations were dramatic and effective, including running a bulldozer into an open pit at the University Washington and organizing 100 protesters to march on the flight apron of Sea-Tac Airport to halt traffic.

These demonstrations precipitated the first federal imposition of Affirmative Action upon local governments and industries. The United States Department of Justice filed suit against unions in late 1969, and in 1970, a broad Affirmative Action program was ordered by the courts in the construction industry.

During the 1980s Scott took his labor and civil rights mission abroad and formed organizations to help laborers in developing countries. [28]

Tyree Scott Apartments are located in Rainier Valley at 4000 Martin Luther King Jr. Way South. A certain number of units are reserved for low-income residents. The others have higher rents and no maximum income requirements.

Samuel J. Smith (1922-1995) served in the
Washington State Legislature for five terms beginning in 1958. Then, in 1967, served five terms as the first Black member of the Seattle City Council. In both of these chambers he promoted civil rights.

Smith was born in Gibsland, Louisiana, and was inspired to go into politics by listening on the radio to President Franklin

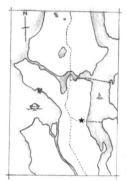

Roosevelt. He came to Seattle via the U. S. Army in 1942. He earned a B.A degree in economics from the University of Washington and worked at Boeing for 17 years.

While serving in the State Legislature, Smith's was a strong voice promoting civil rights. This was also his passion while he served on the Seattle City Council. In 1968, in the wake of the assassination of Martin Luther King Jr., Councilman Smith introduced an ordinance prohibiting racial discrimination in the housing market. The ordinance passed unanimously.

A man of urbane charm, he was known to always answer his phone with "Hello, this is Sam." He was always available to his constituents and spearheaded programs on behalf of the city's racial minorities. He also paved the way for Black and Asian politicians such as Mayor Norm Rice, Governor Gary Locke, and King County Councilman Ron Sims.

In 1985 the Seattle Municipal League honored him as an "Outstanding Public Official." The same year, Governor Booth Gardner designated "Sam Smith Day" in his honor. [30]

Sam Smith Park, dedicated in 1998, comprises the largest part of the I-90 lid and can be accessed at 1400 Martin Luther King Jr. Way South. There are picnic tables, tennis courts, adult exercise equipment, and a sculpture by Gerard Tsutakawa dedicated to children killed by gun violence.

Sam Smith Park
Play Area Picnic Area
Tennis Courts
Bicycle Path

Judge Charles Morehead Stokes

(1903-1996) was elected in 1950 to the Washington State Legislature from the 37th District of central and southeast Seattle. He became King County's first Black state legislator. In 1968 Stokes was the first Black person to be appointed County District Court judge.

While serving in the legislature, Judge Stokes introduced the bill for a state lottery in the 1950s. His co-sponsoring of the Civil Rights Omnibus Bill helped place Washington in the forefront of civil rights legislation.

Born in Fredonia, Kansas, and raised in Pratt, Kansas, Stokes' early life was fraught with misadventure, but as he matured, his life goals were elevated by his decision to become a lawyer. He worked his way through

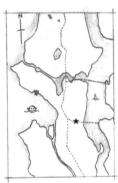

the University of Kansas as a custodian in a girl's dormitory. He played in a jazz band for extra money.

In 1931, Stokes graduated from the University of Kansas Law School but, for lack of money, he did not participate in the graduation ceremonies nor pick up his diploma. He went to Leavenworth, Kansas, and opened his own law practice, but it turned out to be an unsuccessful venture. He came to Seattle in 1943 after learning there was only one Black lawyer in the city.

Charles Stokes was a staunch Republican and served as vice president of the Young Republican National Federation. In 1952 he spoke at the Republican National Convention on behalf of Dwight Eisenhower's candidacy. [31]

Judge Charles M. Stokes Overlook is a pleasant and spacious area on the I-90 Freeway lid with a bicycle path connecting to the freeway. It may be accessed at 20th Avenue South and Judkins, or from Martin Luther King Jr. Way South opposite the entrance to Sam Smith Park. His name was nominated by the Seattle Urban League and the Black Heritage Society. His widow, who occasionally plants flowers there, is pleased that the park is in the neighborhood where they once lived.

Sojourner Truth (1797-1883) was born a slave

in Ulster County, New York. Her first owners were Dutch, and she spoke a Dutch jargon when, at age 9, she was sold to English owners. By 1827, when New York passed an emancipation act, Sojourner Truth had been bought and sold several times, had married, and had borne five children.

Originally named Isabella Van Wagen, or Isabella Baumfree, she changed her name to Sojourner Truth in 1843. This new name would identify her purpose: to travel about and bring people the truth about the Holy Spirit. By this time Truth had moved to New York City, had worked in many menial jobs, and had involved herself in religious movements. She became an itinerant Pentecostal preacher who drew large crowds in evangelistic movements because of her compelling oratory.

As a very spiritual woman, Truth was attracted to Adventist groups and in many instances was one of the few Black women active in them. Through these associations she began to meet feminists and abolitionists such as Frederick Douglass and William Lloyd Garrison. She became excited about their mission and added her fervent and enthusiastic oratory to anti-slavery and feminist causes. Truth was the first Black woman orator to receive wide attention.

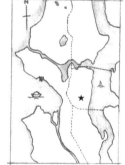

Sojourner Truth's fame spread and, in 1864, she met with President Lincoln. She remained in Washington, D.C., to help improve the living conditions of Black people there and to help escaped slaves from the South to find jobs and housing. Conditions of Black people were so miserable that Truth petitioned Congress for lands in the West to resettle her people. Nothing came of the idea, although she traveled the country seeking support.

In her last years, Truth continued speaking for the rights of women and Black Americans. "Stretch out your hand in brotherhood to the colored people," she said. "We are all the children of one Father in heaven." Sojourner Truth died in Battle Creek, Michigan, and is buried there. [16]

Douglass-Truth Branch Library is located at 23rd Avenue and East Yesler Way. It is the repository of the African American Collection of History and Culture.

Bettylou Valentine (1937-2014) was a civil rights activist,

anthropologist, author, and social worker. Upon arriving in Seattle in 1959 as a student at the University of Washington, she became a founding member of the Congress of Racial Equality (CORE) and volunteered to be its secretary. She was also a national board member of the

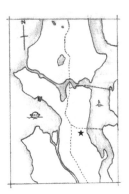

NAACP. When the university would not allow a branch on campus, Valentine became active in the organization of Campus Civil Rights Action Group (CRAG)

Valentine's husband, Charles Valentine, was a professor of anthropology at the University of Washington who authored two studies on the segregation of African Americans in Seattle. Like his wife, Professor Valentine was a member of CORE and was active in civil rights movement. He died 24 hours after picketing in front of Seattle's Federal Office Building.

Mrs. Valentine wrote her Ph.D. thesis on the couple's experience living in an urban ghetto. Her book *Hustling and Hard Work* further develops that theme. She was one of the four authors of *Seattle in Black and White*, which examined racism in Seattle. For 12 years, she was a Commissioner on the Seattle Housing Authority. Her last 16 years of work were spent as director of the Youth and Family Service Organization.

Mrs. Valentine was confined to a wheelchair for a time before she died. She was often seen shopping at the University Village. Her memorial was held at the Masonic Ballroom. [29]

Betty Valentine Center is located at 1901 Martin Luther King Jr. Way South. It provides mental health services as well as youth and family services. Founded in 1976, it began as a nonprofit drug and alcohol treatment center for young people of color who felt alienated. From its beginning in portables in the Mount Baker neighborhood, it moved into its new facility thanks in part to the efforts of Bettylou Valentine.

Florasina Ware (1912-1981) was the quintessential

activist. She was known for raising a strong and logical voice on behalf of children, the elderly, and the poor. She possessed an abiding faith in people's ability to find a better way for the downtrodden. Above all, she was clear-sighted, direct, and forthright in her beliefs.

Born in Fort Worth, Texas, Flo Ware moved about with her family in a specially equipped railroad car provided by the company for which her father worked. Until high school she never went to the same school for more than a few months. She attended college for a short time, married, and moved to Tacoma. She moved to Seattle in 1947.

In the early 1950s, dissatisfied with the quality of Central Area schools, Ware decided to press school officials to work harder for improvements. She was arrested once for passing out leaflets in front of Horace Mann Elementary School. She continually agitated for social change in a calm and positive manner.

Ware was known to be a very secure person with little interest in material possessions. Her high regard for people of all races, religions, and economic classes caused her to devote countless hours to many worthy causes, particularly those relating to education, health, the elderly, and jobs for the poor.

Flo Ware represented Seattle at numerous national conferences on programs from Head Start to support for the aged. She served on innumerable national and local boards and received over 75 awards for her community work. She was an organizer of the Central Area School Board and the Foster Parent Association. She spearheaded the Meals on Wheels Program for the elderly and had a radio talk show from 1968 to 1979 on KRAB.

In addition to community and national activities, Ms. Ware raised 20

foster children and was a mainstay on the Seattle King County Economic Opportunity Board during the War on Poverty years. [16]

Flo Ware Park is located on the corner of 29th Avenue South and South Jackson Street. There are swings and slides for children and a gathering place for the Leschi community.

Dr. James Washington Jr. (1908-2000) was

born in Gloster, Mississippi. He was a painter, a sculptor, and a member of the Northwest School of Artists, which included such luminaries as Mark Tobey and Morris Graves. He began creating art when he was 12 years old under the influence of his family and a Baptist minister. At age 14 he apprenticed to become a shoemaker. He became involved in the Federal Works Project Administration (WPA) when he was 29 and worked as an assistant art instructor at Baptist Academy in Vicksburg, Mississippi. Washington organized the first WPA sponsored exhibition for Black artists in the state.

In 1941, Washington moved to Little Rock, Arkansas, where his mother was living and began repairing shoes at Camp Robinson. Since this was a federal Civil Service job, he was able to relocate to Bremerton, where he worked in electrical wiring on naval warships based there. Transferring to Fort Lawton in Seattle, he set up and operated a shoe shop.

During this time, Washington and his wife Rogella bought a home in Seattle's Madison Valley neighborhood, where he maintained a studio. He quickly became a part of Seattle's art community with exhibits at Frederick and Nelson's Department Store and Mt. Zion Baptist Church. It was during a trip to Mexico that he found volcanic stone that soon inspired him into the work of sculpture. Washington's first stone sculpture was entitled *Young Boy of Athens*. Some of his sculptures can be found at Odessa Brown Children's Clinic and Mt. Zion Baptist Church.

Washington's art expressed his spirituality and drew on religious themes as in his series of paintings of the *Passover, the Nativity* and *Christ in the Garden of Gethsemane*. He also worked on African American subjects including a sculpture of Jomo Kenyatta and six sculptures of famous African Americans for a plaza in Philadelphia. [32, 33]

Dr. James Washington Jr's Home is located at 1816 26th Avenue, where he and his wife Rogella lived for more than 50 years. It is a museum and cultural center with a studio available for future artists. It was designated a historical landmark by Seattle Landmarks Preservation Board in recognition of Dr. Washington's significant contributions to the history and culture of the city of Seattle.

Phillis Wheatley (1753-1784) was the first

Black woman to publish a book of poems despite having spent much of her life as a slave. She was born in Gambia, Africa, and after being captured by slave traders, she was brought to America in 1761. Fortunately, she was bought by the Wheatley family in Boston. Her first name was derived from the ship that she came on.

Educated by the Wheatley family, in a little over a year she could read the Bible, Greek and Latin classics, and British literature. Ms. Wheatley also studied astronomy and geography. By the time she was 14 she began writing poetry. Her first poem was published in 1767. In 1771, she traveled to London with a Wheatley son to publish her first collection of poems, *Poems on Various Subjects, Religious and Moral.* The book included her portrait to prove that the poems were written by a Black woman.

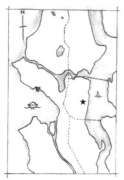

After her emancipation, Wheatley became involved in the anti-slavery movement. Much of her poetry was religious and both enslavers and abolitionists read her work. The abolitionists used it to prove that people of color had intellect and it helped the cause of their movement.

She married a free Black man from Boston in 1778, and had three children but none survived. She wrote a second book of poems but was unable to have it published. Phillis Wheatley worked as a scrubwoman to support her family and continued to write. She died from complications during childbirth. [34]

YWCA Phillis Wheatley Branch is located at 2920 East Cherry Street and houses administrative offices and a variety of programs, including a food bank, housing, and domestic-violence support.

Lenny Wilkens (b. 1937) was a memorable

basketball player in the 1960s and 1970s. He played with
the Seattle SuperSonics and later served as their coach,
winning an NBA Championship for Seattle in 1979, and
bringing glory to the city. Other teams Wilkens played
on included the St. Louis Hawks, Cleveland Cavaliers, and
Portland Trail Blazers.

Born in Brooklyn, New York, son of an Irish American mother and an
African American father, Wilkens received a scholarship to play basketball
at Providence College, a small Catholic institution in Rhode Island.
After graduation, Wilkens played for the St. Louis Hawks and was such a
valuable player that he was voted nine times to NBA All-Star teams. He
played briefly with the Sonics and then came back to coach in the 1977-

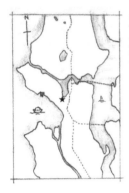

1978 season. By that season's end he had led them to the
NBA Finals. Wilkens was named one of the 50 greatest
players by the NBA and one of the top coaches in league
history. He was inducted into the Naismith Hall of Fame
as a player and a coach.

Wilkens lives in Seattle and is the founder and chair
of the Lenny Wilkens Foundation for children, where
he raised over $7.5 million for the Odessa Brown
Children's Clinic. Lenny Wilkens is also involved in other
organizations that provide care and opportunities for
local disadvantaged youth. For his social progress effort,
Wilkens was conferred the Doctor of Humanities by
Providence College and Seattle University. [35]

Lenny Wilkens Way is located on Thomas Street between 1st Avenue
North and 2nd Avenue North near the original site of the Seattle
Coliseum—now Climate Pledge Arena—where Wilkens brought

basketball glory to the
city. The honorific was
approved by the city council
in September 2021 after
being sponsored by Alex
Pedersen.

References

1. Acox, Clarence: https://www.Blackpast.org//african-american-history/acox-jr-clarence-1947

2. Anderson, Ernestine: https://www.Blackpast.org/?s=ernestine+anderson

3. Ball, Alice: https://sop.washington.edu/uwsop-alumni-legend-alice-ball-class-of-1914-solved-leprosy-riddle/

4. Ball, Alice: https://www.biography.com/scientist/alice-ball

5. Byrd Barr, Roberta: Mary T. Henry. "Roberta Byrd Barr, 1919-1993," HistoryLink, November 9, 1998, https://www.historylink.org/File/306

6. Cayton, Horace: Mary T. Henry, "Cayton, Horace (1859-1940)," HistoryLink, November 9, 1998, https://www.historylink.org/File/309

7. Clark, Patricia: https://trellis.law/judge/patricia.h.clark

8. Dewitty, Thelma: Mary T. Henry, "Thelma Dewitty, 1912-1977," HistoryLink, November 10, 1998, https://www.historylink.org/File/1163

9. Eng, Lily "Jean Shy Farris showed spicey dramatic flair throughout her life," The Seattle Times, December 4, 1992

10. Gayton, Carver: Carver Gayton, "Gayton, Carver Clark (b. 1938)," HistoryLink, May 28, 2004, https://www.historylink.org/File/4305

11. Gayton, Gary: Alyssa Burrows, "Gayton Gary David (b. 1933)," HistoryLink, February 28, 2003, https://www.historylink.org/File/3714

12. Gayton, Guela: Mary T. Henry, "Guela Gayton Johnson, (1927-2018)," HistoryLink, August 28, 2018, https://www.historylink.org/File/9459

13. Gayton, Willetta: Mary T. Henry, "Willetta Gayton, (1909-1991)," HistoryLink, April 29, 2010, https://www.historylink.org/File/9413

14. Gossett, Larry: https://www.Blackpast.org/african-american-history/gossett-larry-1945

15. Harris, Homer: Mary T. Henry, "Harris, Dr. Homer E. Jr. (1916-2007)," HistoryLink, July 17, 2003, https://www.historylink.org/File/4222

16. Henry, Mary T. Tribute: Seattle Public Places Named for Black People (Seattle: Statice Press, 1997)

17. Hunt, Denice: https://qahistory.org/denice-johnson-hunt/

18. Jones, Quincy: https://www.Blackpast.org/african-american-history/jones-quincy-1933

19. Kelly, Sam: https://www.Blackpast.org/african-american-history/people-african-american-history/kelly-samuel-eugene-1926-2009/

20. Lawrence, Jacob: https://www.biography.com/artist/jacob-lawrence

21. Lawson, Jacqueline: https://www.Blackpast.org/author/lawsonjacqueline/

22. Lewis, John: https://www.bbc.com/news/world-us-canada-53454169

23. Lincoln, Abbey: https://www.Blackpast.org/african-american-history/lincoln-abbey-1930-2010

24. Little, John: https://parkways.seattle.gov/2016/04/12/about-the-john-c-little-sr-spirit-award/

25. McKinney, Louise: https://www.Blackpast.org/?s=Louise+McKinney

26. McKinney, Samuel: https://www.Blackpast.org/african-american-history/mckinney-samuel-berry-1926-0/

27. Peoples, Gertrude: Mary T. Henry, "Gertrude Johnson Peoples (b. 1932)," HistoryLink, May 31, 2012, https://www.historylink.org/File/10093

28. Scott, Tyree: Mary T. Henry, "Tyree Scott, (1940-2003)," HistoryLink, July 24, 2007, https://www.historylink.org/File/8222

29. Singler, Joan: Seattle in Black and White: The Congress of Racial Equality and the Fight for Equal Opportunity (Seattle: University of Washington Press, 2011)

30. Smith, Sam: https://www.Blackpast.org/?s=sam+smith

31. Stokes, Charles M.: Mary T. Henry, "Charles Moorehead Stokes (1903-1990)," HistoryLink, January 9, 1999, https://www.historylink.org/File/674

32. Washington, James: https://www.Blackpast.org/?s=James+Washington

33. Washington, James: https://www.whereweconverge.com/post/dr-james-washington-jr-statue-unveiling

34. Wheatley, Phillis: https://www.Blackpast.org/?s=Phillis+Wheatley

35. Wilkens, Lenny: https://www.Blackpast.org/african-american-history/wilkens-lenny-1937

CPSIA information can be obtained
at www.ICGtesting.com
Printed in the USA
LVHW071254170723
752375LV00008B/154